Festival Of Taste: Indian Recipes

Henry Zothanmawia

Published by Golden Leaf Haven Publishing, 2024.

Festival Of Taste: Indian Recipes

© Copyright 2024, Henry Zothanmawia

Published 2024 by Golden Leaf Haven Publishing, 36 Saint John's Place, Freeport 11520-4618, New York, USA

Airhub 1425, UBX 6 Poyle Trading Estate, Colndale Road, Colnbrook, Slough SL30AA Berkshire, United Kingdom

Table of Contents

Preface

Welcome to "Festival of Taste," a vibrant and diverse collection of Indian recipes that celebrates the rich culinary heritage of this incredible country. India's cuisine is a true reflection of its cultural tapestry, woven from threads of tradition, regional flair, and timeless techniques.

As you embark on this gastronomic journey, you'll discover the bold flavors, aromas, and textures that define Indian cooking. From spicy curries to delicate biryanis, and from crispy street food to indulgent desserts, every dish tells a story of India's remarkable diversity.

This cookbook is a labor of love, born from my passion for cooking and sharing the joys of Indian cuisine. As a finance professional turned food enthusiast, I've had the privilege of exploring India's culinary landscape and learning from its master chefs, home cooks, and street food artisans.

Within these pages, you'll find:
Authentic Indian recipes, carefully curated from across the regions
Step-by-step instructions to guide you
India's culinary ingredients, and cooking techniques
Tips and variations to inspire your creativity

Whether you're a seasoned cook or just starting your culinary adventure, "A Festival of Taste" invites you to experience the warmth, hospitality, and love that Indian food embodies.

Join me on this delicious journey, and let's celebrate the festival of taste that Indian cuisine has to offer!

Happy cooking!
Henry Zothanmawia

About the Author

Henry Zothanmawia is a multifaceted individual whose passion for cooking knows no bounds. By profession, he is a seasoned expert in the financial institution, with years of experience in navigating the complexities of the industry. However, his true love and creative outlet lies in the culinary world.

Born and raised in India, Henry was exposed to the rich and diverse flavors of Indian cuisine from a young age. His love for cooking was nurtured by his family, who encouraged him to experiment with traditional recipes and ingredients. As he grew older, Henry's interest in cooking only deepened, and he began to explore the various regional cuisines of India.

Despite his demanding career in finance, Henry always found solace in cooking. He would often spend his weekends experimenting with new recipes, techniques, and ingredients. His friends and family were more than happy to serve as guinea pigs, and soon, word of his culinary prowess spread.

As Henry's passion for cooking continued to grow, he decided to share his love with a wider audience. This cookbook is a culmination of his culinary journey, featuring a collection of traditional Indian recipes with a modern twist.

Inspiration and Philosophy
Henry's cooking philosophy is simple: to create dishes that are not only delicious but also authentic and accessible. He believes that Indian

cuisine is more than just a collection of recipes; it's a reflection of the country's rich cultural heritage.

Through this cookbook, Henry aims to inspire home cooks to explore the diverse flavors of India. He shares his expertise and techniques, garnered from years of experimentation and research, to demystify complex recipes and make them accessible to cooks of all levels.

Personal Touch

What sets Henry's cookbook apart is the personal touch he brings to each recipe. From anecdotes about his childhood to tips and tricks learned from his family, Henry's love for cooking shines through on every page.

As you journey through this cookbook, you'll discover Henry's favorite recipes, each one carefully crafted to showcase the diversity and richness of Indian cuisine. From classic dishes like Chole Bhature to regional specialties like Mizoram's Bai, every recipe is a testament to Henry's passion for cooking.

A Message from the Author

I'm thrilled to share my love for Indian cuisine with you through this cookbook. Cooking is not just about following a recipe; it's about sharing love, culture, and tradition. I hope this book inspires you to explore the rich flavors of India and creates memories that will last a lifetime.

Pakoda

Pakoda, a popular Indian snack, is a delicious and crunchy fried fritter made with gram flour (besan) and vegetables. Here's a simple recipe to make pakoda at home:

Ingredients:
1 cup gram flour (besan)
1/2 cup chopped onions
1/2 cup chopped cauliflower
1/2 cup chopped potatoes
1/4 cup chopped cilantro
1/4 cup chili powder
1/4 cup garam masala
1/4 cup salt
1/4 cup lemon juice
1/4 cup water
Oil for frying

Instructions:
1. In a large bowl, mix gram flour, chili powder, garam masala, and salt.
2. Add chopped onions, cauliflower, potatoes, and cilantro. Mix well.
3. Gradually add lemon juice and water, mixing until a thick batter forms.
4. Heat oil in a deep frying pan over medium heat.
5. Using a spoon, drop small portions of the batter into the oil.
6. Fry pakodas until golden brown, turning occasionally (5-7 minutes).
7. Remove pakodas from oil, drain excess oil on paper towels.

8. Serve hot with chutney or raita.

Tips:
Use a thermometer to maintain oil temperature (350°F).
Don't overcrowd the pan; fry in batches.
Adjust chili powder for desired spiciness.
Experiment with different vegetables (e.g., carrots, bell peppers).
For a healthier option, bake pakodas at 400°F (20-25 minutes).

Variations:
Palak Pakoda: Add spinach puree to the batter.
Paneer Pakoda: Add crumbled paneer (Indian cheese).
Mixed Vegetable Pakoda: Use various vegetables.

Nutritional Information (approximate):

Per serving (4-6 pakodas):
Calories: 250-375
Protein: 5-7g
Fat: 10-15g
Carbohydrates: 30-40g
Fiber: 2-3g

Jhal Muri

Jhal Muri is a popular Bengali street food, a spicy and flavorful puffed rice snack. Here's a simple recipe to make Jhal Muri at home:

Ingredients:
2 cups puffed rice (muri)
1/2 cup chopped onions
1/2 cup chopped tomatoes
1/4 cup chopped cilantro
1/4 cup mustard oil or vegetable oil
1/4 cup lemon juice
1 tablespoon Bengali mustard paste (or Dijon mustard)
1 teaspoon grated ginger
1 teaspoon cumin seeds
Salt, to taste
Chili powder, to taste
Optional: chopped chilies, peanuts, or sesame seeds

Instructions:
1. Heat oil in a pan over medium heat.
2. Add cumin seeds and let them sizzle.
3. Add chopped onions, tomatoes, and cilantro. Saute until onions are translucent.
4. Add mustard paste, ginger, salt, and chili powder. Mix well.
5. Add puffed rice and stir until evenly coated with the spice mixture.
6. Squeeze lemon juice and mix.
7. Taste and adjust seasoning.

8. Serve immediately.

Tips:
Use fresh puffed rice for best results.
Adjust chili powder to desired spiciness.
Add chopped chilies for extra heat.
Mix in peanuts or sesame seeds for crunch.
Experiment with different oils (e.g., coconut, olive).

Variations:
Classic Jhal Muri: Add chopped boiled potatoes.
Spicy Jhal Muri: Increase chili powder or add chopped green chilies.
Mumbai Style Jhal Muri: Add sev (fried gram flour noodles).

Nutritional Information (approximate):

Per serving:
Calories: 150-200
Protein: 2-3g
Fat: 5-7g
Carbohydrates: 25-30g
Fiber: 2-3g

Bhel Puri

Bhel Puri is a popular Indian street food, a flavorful and crunchy snack made with puffed rice, vegetables, and chutneys. Here's a simple recipe to make Bhel Puri at home:

Ingredients:
2 cups puffed rice (murmura or mamra)
1 cup boiled and diced potatoes
1 cup diced onions
1 cup diced tomatoes
1/2 cup chopped cilantro
1/4 cup tamarind chutney
1/4 cup green chutney
1/4 cup date and tamarind chutney (optional)
1/4 cup sev (fried gram flour noodles)
1/4 cup chopped peanuts or almonds (optional)
Salt, to taste
Lemon juice, to taste
Oil, for frying

Instructions:
1. Heat oil in a pan and fry sev until crispy. Drain excess oil.
2. In a large bowl, mix puffed rice, boiled potatoes, onions, tomatoes, and cilantro.
3. Add tamarind chutney, green chutney, and date and tamarind chutney (if using). Mix well.
4. Add fried sev, peanuts or almonds (if using), and salt. Mix.

5. Squeeze lemon juice and mix.
6. Taste and adjust seasoning.
7. Serve immediately.

Tips:
Use fresh puffed rice for best results.
Adjust chutney quantities to desired sweetness and spiciness.
Add chopped chilies or chili powder for extra heat.
Experiment with different nuts or seeds (e.g., cashews, pumpkin seeds).

Variations:
Mumbai style Bhel Puri: Add diced mango or pineapple.
Delhi style Bhel Puri: Add boiled chickpeas or yogurt.
Spicy Bhel Puri: Increase chili powder or add chopped green chilies.

Nutritional Information (approximate):

Per serving:
Calories: 250-300
Protein: 5-7g
Fat: 10-12g
Carbohydrates: 35-40g
Fiber: 3-4g

Chatpate

Chatpate, also known as Chatpata, is a popular Indian street food snack originating from the eastern regions of India, particularly in Bengal and Odisha. This flavorful and spicy snack is made with a mixture of boiled chickpeas, onions, tomatoes, and chutneys.

Ingredients:
1 cup boiled chickpeas
1/2 cup diced onions
1/2 cup diced tomatoes
1/4 cup chopped cilantro
2 tablespoons mustard oil or vegetable oil
1 tablespoon Bengali mustard paste (or Dijon mustard)
1 teaspoon grated ginger
1 teaspoon cumin seeds
1/2 teaspoon chili powder
Salt, to taste
2 tablespoons tamarind chutney
1 tablespoon green chutney
Lemon juice, to taste
Optional: chopped chilies, peanuts, or sesame seeds

Instructions:
1. Heat oil in a pan over medium heat.
2. Add cumin seeds and let them sizzle.
3. Add chopped onions, tomatoes, and cilantro. Saute until onions are translucent.

4. Add mustard paste, ginger, chili powder, and salt. Mix well.
5. Add boiled chickpeas and stir until coated with the spice mixture.
6. Add tamarind chutney and green chutney. Mix.
7. Squeeze lemon juice and mix.
8. Taste and adjust seasoning.
9. Serve immediately.

Tips:
Use fresh chickpeas for best results.
Adjust chili powder to desired spiciness.
Add chopped chilies for extra heat.
Experiment with different oils (e.g., coconut, olive).
Mix in peanuts or sesame seeds for crunch.

Variations:
Classic Chatpate: Add chopped boiled potatoes.
Spicy Chatpate: Increase chili powder or add chopped green chilies.
Mumbai style Chatpate: Add sev (fried gram flour noodles).

Nutritional Information (approximate):

Per serving:
Calories: 200-250
Protein: 10-12g
Fat: 8-10g
Carbohydrates: 25-30g
Fiber: 4-5g

Singju

Singju is a popular Manipuri street food, a flavorful and spicy salad made with a variety of ingredients. This refreshing snack is a staple in Manipur, India, and is often served as a side dish or light meal.

Ingredients:
1 cup chopped cabbage
1 cup chopped cucumber
1 cup chopped carrots
1/2 cup chopped onions
1/2 cup chopped coriander
1/4 cup chopped chili peppers
1/4 cup roasted peanuts or sesame seeds
2 tablespoons fermented fish paste (optional)
2 tablespoons chili powder
1 tablespoon ginger paste
Salt, to taste
Lemon juice, to taste
Oil, for frying

Instructions:
1. Heat oil in a pan and fry peanuts or sesame seeds until crispy.
2. In a large bowl, mix chopped cabbage, cucumber, carrots, onions, coriander, and chili peppers.
3. Add fermented fish paste (if using), chili powder, ginger paste, and salt. Mix well.
4. Squeeze lemon juice and mix.

5. Add fried peanuts or sesame seeds and mix.
6. Taste and adjust seasoning.
7. Serve immediately.

Tips:

Use fresh vegetables for best results.

Adjust chili powder to desired spiciness.

Add protein sources like boiled chickpeas or tofu.

Experiment with different nuts or seeds (e.g., almonds, pumpkin seeds).

Omit fermented fish paste for a vegetarian version.

Variations:

Traditional Singju: Add fermented fish paste.

Vegetarian Singju: Omit fish paste and add tofu.

Spicy Singju: Increase chili powder.

Nutritional Information (approximate):

Per serving:
Calories: 150-200
Protein: 5-7g
Fat: 8-10g
Carbohydrates: 20-25g
Fiber: 3-4g

Note: *Singju is a traditional Manipuri recipe, and the ingredients may vary depending on the region and personal preferences.*

Uruk

Uruk is a popular Assamese snack, a flavorful and spicy fritter made with rice flour, vegetables, and spices. This crispy and crunchy snack is a staple in Assam, India, and is often served as a teatime accompaniment.

Ingredients:
2 cups rice flour
1/2 cup chopped onions
1/2 cup chopped cabbage
1/4 cup chopped coriander
1/4 cup grated ginger
1/4 cup chili powder
1/4 cup salt
1/4 cup water
Oil, for frying

Instructions:
1. Mix rice flour, onions, cabbage, coriander, ginger, chili powder, and salt in a bowl.
2. Gradually add water and mix until a thick batter forms.
3. Heat oil in a deep frying pan over medium heat.
4. Using a spoon, drop small portions of the batter into the oil.
5. Fry uruk until golden brown, turning occasionally (5-7 minutes).
6. Remove uruk from oil, drain excess oil on paper towels.
7. Serve hot with tea or chutney.

Tips:

Use fine rice flour for crispy uruk.
Adjust chili powder to desired spiciness.
Add chopped potatoes or cauliflower for extra texture.
Experiment with different oils (e.g., coconut, mustard).

Variations:
Traditional Uruk: Add fermented rice paste.
Spicy Uruk: Increase chili powder.
Vegetable Uruk: Add grated carrots or zucchini.

Nutritional Information (approximate):

Per serving (4-6 uruk):
Calories: 200-250
Protein: 2-3g
Fat: 10-12g
Carbohydrates: 25-30g
Fiber: 2-3g

Bombay Duck

Bombay Duck, also known as Bombil, is a popular Indian fish fry dish originating from the coastal regions of Maharashtra. This flavorful and crispy fish fry is made with dried Bombay duck fish, marinated in spices and herbs.

Ingredients:
4-6 dried Bombay duck fish (or fresh fish)
1/2 cup gram flour (besan)
1/4 cup lemon juice
1/4 cup ginger paste
1/4 cup garlic paste
1 tablespoon chili powder
1 teaspoon cumin powder
1 teaspoon coriander powder
Salt, to taste
Oil, for frying
Chopped cilantro, for garnish

Instructions:

Marination:
1. Clean and cut the fish into small pieces.
2. Mix gram flour, lemon juice, ginger paste, garlic paste, chili powder, cumin powder, coriander powder, and salt.
3. Apply the marinade to the fish pieces and refrigerate for 30 minutes.

Frying:
1. Heat oil in a deep frying pan over medium heat.
2. Remove fish from marinade, allowing excess to drip off.
3. Fry fish until golden brown, turning occasionally (5-7 minutes).
4. Remove fish from oil, drain excess oil on paper towels.

Garnish and Serve:
1. Garnish with chopped cilantro.
2. Serve hot with rice, roti, or as a snack.

Tips:
Use fresh fish for best results.
Adjust chili powder to desired spiciness.
Add chopped onions or tomatoes to the marinade.
Experiment with different oils (e.g., coconut, olive).

Variations:
Traditional Bombay Duck: Use dried fish.
Spicy Bombay Duck: Increase chili powder.
Tandoori Bombay Duck: Add yogurt and tandoori masala.

Nutritional Information (approximate):

Per serving (4-6 pieces):
Calories: 250-300
Protein: 20-25g
Fat: 10-12g
Carbohydrates: 10-15g
Fiber: 2-3g

Ghugni Chaat

Ghugni Chaat is a beloved Indian street food, originating from Eastern India, particularly in West Bengal and Odisha. This flavorful and spicy snack is made with boiled yellow peas or chickpeas, onions, tomatoes, and a blend of spices.

Ingredients:
1 cup boiled yellow peas or chickpeas
1/2 cup diced onions
1/2 cup diced tomatoes
1/4 cup chopped cilantro
1/4 cup tamarind chutney
1/4 cup green chutney
1 tablespoon mustard oil or vegetable oil
1 teaspoon cumin seeds
1 teaspoon coriander powder
1/2 teaspoon chili powder
Salt, to taste
Lemon juice, to taste

Instructions:
1. Heat oil in a pan over medium heat.
2. Add cumin seeds and let them sizzle.
3. Add diced onions and sauté until translucent.
4. Add diced tomatoes and cook until soft.
5. Add boiled peas or chickpeas, coriander powder, chili powder, and salt. Mix well.

6. Add tamarind chutney and green chutney. Mix.
7. Squeeze lemon juice and mix.
8. Garnish with chopped cilantro.
9. Serve immediately.

Tips:
Use fresh peas or chickpeas for best results.
Adjust chili powder to desired spiciness.
Add chopped potatoes or cauliflower for extra texture.
Experiment with different oils (e.g., coconut, olive).

Variations:
Classic Ghugni: Use boiled yellow peas.
Chickpea Ghugni: Use boiled chickpeas.
Spicy Ghugni: Increase chili powder.

Nutritional Information (approximate):

Per serving:
Calories: 200-250
Protein: 10-12g
Fat: 8-10g
Carbohydrates: 25-30g
Fiber: 4-5g

Dahi Bhalle

Dahi Bhalle, also known as Dahi Vada, is a beloved Indian street food consisting of crispy fried lentil dumplings soaked in yogurt and spices.

Ingredients:

For Bhalle:
1 cup split black gram (urad dal)
1/2 cup split green gram (moong dal)
1/4 cup chopped onions
1/4 cup chopped cilantro
1/4 cup grated ginger
1/4 cup chili powder
Salt, to taste
Oil, for frying

For Dahi:
1 cup yogurt
1/4 cup chopped cilantro
1/4 cup chopped mint
1 tablespoon cumin powder
1 tablespoon coriander powder
1/2 teaspoon chili powder
Salt, to taste
1 tablespoon lemon juice

Instructions:

Bhalle:
1. Soak dal for 4-5 hours.
2. Grind dal into a paste.
3. Add onions, cilantro, ginger, chili powder, and salt. Mix.
4. Shape into small dumplings.
5. Fry until golden brown.

Dahi:
1. Mix yogurt, cilantro, mint, cumin powder, coriander powder, chili powder, and salt.
2. Add lemon juice and mix.

Assembly:
1. Soak fried bhalle in water for 10-15 minutes.
2. Squeeze excess water from bhalle.
3. Dip bhalle in dahi mixture.
4. Garnish with cilantro, chili powder, and cumin powder.

Tips:
Use fresh yogurt for best results.
Adjust chili powder to desired spiciness.
Add chopped chilies or garlic for extra flavor.
Experiment with different spices (e.g., garam masala, chaat masala).

Variations:
Classic Dahi Bhalle: Use split black gram.
Moong Dal Bhalle: Use split green gram.
Spicy Dahi Bhalle: Increase chili powder.

Nutritional Information (approximate):

Per serving (4-6 bhalle):
Calories: 250-300
Protein: 10-12g
Fat: 10-12g
Carbohydrates: 30-35g
Fiber: 4-5g

Pani Puri

Pani Puri, also known as Golgappas or Puchkas, is a beloved Indian street food consisting of crispy puris filled with flavored water, tamarind chutney, and various fillings.

Ingredients:

For Puri:
2 cups all purpose flour
1/2 cup semolina
1/4 cup ghee or oil
1/4 cup lukewarm water
Salt, to taste

For Pani (Flavored Water):
1 liter water
1/2 cup tamarind paste
1/4 cup green chutney
1/4 cup lemon juice
1/4 cup chili powder
Salt, to taste
Ice cubes

For Fillings:
Boiled and mashed chickpeas
Boiled and diced potatoes
Chopped onions

Chopped cilantro
Sev (fried gram flour noodles)
Tamarind chutney

Instructions:

Puri:
1. Mix flour, semolina, and salt.
2. Add ghee or oil and mix.
3. Gradually add lukewarm water and knead.
4. Rest dough for 30 minutes.
5. Roll out dough and cut into small circles.
6. Fry puris until crispy.

Pani:
1. Mix water, tamarind paste, green chutney, lemon juice, chili powder, and salt.
2. Chill in the refrigerator.

Assembly:
1. Fill puris with chickpeas, potatoes, onions, and cilantro.
2. Add sev and tamarind chutney.
3. Fill with flavored water.
4. Serve immediately.

Tips:
Use fresh ingredients for best results.
Adjust chili powder to desired spiciness.
Experiment with different fillings (e.g., boiled moong sprouts).
Use a flavorful oil (e.g., mustard oil) for frying puris.

Variations:

Classic Pani Puri: Use tamarind paste.

Spicy Pani Puri: Increase chili powder.

Mumbai style Pani Puri: Add garlic chutney.

Nutritional Information (approximate):

Per serving (4-6 puris):

Calories: 200-250

Protein: 5-7g

Fat: 10-12g

Carbohydrates: 25-30g

Fiber: 3-4g

Regional Variations:

Pani Puri (Mumbai)

Golgappas (Delhi)

Puchkas (Kolkata)

Samosa

Samosa is a popular Indian snack consisting of crispy fried or baked pastries filled with spiced potatoes, peas, and onions.

Ingredients:

For Dough:
2 cups all purpose flour
1 teaspoon salt
1/4 teaspoon baking powder
1/4 cup ghee or oil
1/2 cup lukewarm water

For Filling:
2 large boiled and mashed potatoes
1 cup peas
1/2 cup chopped onions
1/4 cup chopped cilantro
1/4 cup ghee or oil
1 teaspoon cumin seeds
1 teaspoon coriander powder
1/2 teaspoon garam masala
1/2 teaspoon chili powder
Salt, to taste

Instructions:

Dough:
1. Mix flour, salt, and baking powder.
2. Add ghee or oil and mix.
3. Gradually add lukewarm water and knead.
4. Rest dough for 30 minutes.

Filling:
1. Heat ghee or oil in a pan.
2. Add cumin seeds and let them sizzle.
3. Add onions, peas, coriander powder, garam masala, chili powder, and salt. Cook until onions are translucent.
4. Mix in mashed potatoes and cilantro.

Assembly:
1. Divide dough into small balls.
2. Roll out each ball into a thin circle.
3. Place filling in the center.
4. Fold and seal samosa.
5. Fry until golden brown or bake at 375°F (190°C) for 15-20 minutes.

Tips:
Use fresh ingredients for best results.
Adjust chili powder to desired spiciness.
Experiment with different fillings (e.g., lentils, cauliflower).
Use a flavorful oil (e.g., mustard oil) for frying.

Variations:
Classic Samosa: Use potatoes and peas.
Spicy Samosa: Increase chili powder.
Baked Samosa: Bake instead of frying.

Nutritional Information (approximate):

Per serving (4-6 samosas):
Calories: 250-300
Protein: 5-7g
Fat: 10-12g
Carbohydrates: 30-35g
Fiber: 3-4g

Regional Variations:
Samosa (North India)
Singara (East India)
Sambusa (South India)

Chole Bhature

Chole Bhature is a beloved Indian breakfast dish consisting of spicy chickpea curry (Chole) served with deep fried puffed bread (Bhature).

Ingredients:

For Chole:
1 cup chickpeas (chana)
2 medium onions, chopped
2 medium tomatoes, chopped
1 teaspoon cumin seeds
1 teaspoon coriander powder
1 teaspoon garam masala
1/2 teaspoon turmeric
1/2 teaspoon red chili powder
Salt, to taste
2 tablespoons oil
2 tablespoons lemon juice

For Bhature:
2 cups all purpose flour
1 teaspoon salt
1/4 teaspoon baking powder
1/4 cup yogurt
1/4 cup ghee or oil
Water, as needed

Instructions:

Chole:
1. Soak chickpeas overnight.
2. Boil chickpeas until tender.
3. Heat oil in a pan.
4. Add cumin seeds, onions, and tomatoes. Cook until onions are translucent.
5. Add coriander powder, garam masala, turmeric, chili powder, and salt. Mix.
6. Add boiled chickpeas, lemon juice, and water. Simmer.

Bhature:
1. Mix flour, salt, and baking powder.
2. Add yogurt, ghee or oil, and water. Knead.
3. Rest dough for 30 minutes.
4. Divide dough into small balls.
5. Roll out each ball into a circle.
6. Fry until puffed and golden.

Assembly:
1. Serve Chole with Bhature.
2. Garnish with chopped cilantro, onion, and lemon wedges.

Tips:
Use fresh chickpeas for best results.
Adjust chili powder to desired spiciness.
Experiment with different spices (e.g., amchur powder).
Use a flavorful oil (e.g., mustard oil) for frying.

Variations:

Classic Chole Bhature: Use chickpeas and Bhature.
Spicy Chole Bhature: Increase chili powder.
Vegan Chole Bhature: Replace ghee with oil.

Nutritional Information (approximate):

Per serving (4-6 servings):
Calories: 400-500
Protein: 15-20g
Fat: 20-25g
Carbohydrates: 40-50g
Fiber: 5-7g

Biryani

Biryani is a beloved Indian mixed rice dish made with aromatic spices, basmati rice, and marinated meat or vegetables.

Ingredients:

For Basmati Rice:
2 cups basmati rice
4 cups water
1 tablespoon ghee or oil
1 teaspoon salt

For Marinade:
1 pound boneless chicken or lamb
1/2 cup yogurt
2 tablespoons lemon juice
2 tablespoons ginger paste
2 tablespoons garlic paste
1 teaspoon cumin powder
1 teaspoon coriander powder
1/2 teaspoon turmeric
1/2 teaspoon red chili powder
Salt, to taste

For Biryani Masala:
2 tablespoons coriander seeds
1 tablespoon cumin seeds

1 tablespoon cinnamon sticks
1 tablespoon cardamom powder
1/2 teaspoon mace powder
1/2 teaspoon nutmeg powder

For Layering:
2 tablespoons ghee or oil
Chopped cilantro, for garnish

Instructions:

Basmati Rice:
1. Rinse rice and soak for 30 minutes.
2. Boil water, add ghee or oil, and salt.
3. Drain rice and add to boiling water.
4. Cook until rice is 70% done.

Marinade:
1. Mix yogurt, lemon juice, ginger paste, garlic paste, cumin powder, coriander powder, turmeric, chili powder, and salt.
2. Add marinade to chicken or lamb and refrigerate for 30 minutes.

Biryani Masala:
1. Dry roast coriander seeds, cumin seeds, cinnamon sticks, cardamom powder, mace powder, and nutmeg powder.
2. Grind into a fine powder.

Layering:
1. Heat ghee or oil in a pan.
2. Add marinated meat or vegetables and cook until browned.
3. Layer cooked rice, meat or vegetables, and Biryani Masala in a pot.

4. Repeat layering process.
5. Cover and cook on low heat for 10-15 minutes.

Assembly:
1. Garnish with chopped cilantro.
2. Serve hot.

Tips:

Use high quality basmati rice.
Adjust chili powder to desired spiciness.
Experiment with different proteins (e.g., shrimp, tofu).
Use a flavorful oil (e.g., ghee, mustard oil).

Variations:

Hyderabadi Biryani: Use lamb and add saffron.
Lucknowi Biryani: Use chicken and add potatoes.
Vegetable Biryani: Replace meat with vegetables.

Nutritional Information (approximate):

Per serving (4-6 servings):
Calories: 500-600
Protein: 25-30g
Fat: 20-25g
Carbohydrates: 60-70g
Fiber: 5-7g

Pulao

Pulao is a popular Indian rice dish made with aromatic spices, basmati rice, and mixed vegetables or meat.

Ingredients:

For Basmati Rice:
2 cups basmati rice
4 cups water
1 tablespoon ghee or oil
1 teaspoon salt

For Pulao Masala:
1 teaspoon cumin seeds
1 teaspoon coriander seeds
1/2 teaspoon cinnamon powder
1/2 teaspoon cardamom powder
1/4 teaspoon mace powder
1/4 teaspoon nutmeg powder

For Mixed Vegetables (optional):
1 cup peas
1 cup carrots, diced
1 cup cauliflower, florets
1/2 cup onions, chopped
1/2 cup bell peppers, chopped

For Meat (optional):
1 pound boneless chicken or lamb, diced

Instructions:

Basmati Rice:
1. Rinse rice and soak for 30 minutes.
2. Boil water, add ghee or oil, and salt.
3. Drain rice and add to boiling water.
4. Cook until rice is 70% done.

Pulao Masala:
1. Dry roast cumin seeds, coriander seeds, cinnamon powder, cardamom powder, mace powder, and nutmeg powder.
2. Grind into a fine powder.

Vegetable or Meat Preparation:
1. Heat oil in a pan.
2. Add onions and sauté until translucent.
3. Add mixed vegetables or meat and cook until tender.

Assembly:
1. Heat ghee or oil in a large pan.
2. Add Pulao Masala and sauté for 1 minute.
3. Add cooked rice, mixed vegetables or meat, and salt.
4. Mix well.
5. Cook for 5-7 minutes.

Tips:
Use high quality basmati rice.
Adjust spice level to desired taste.

Experiment with different vegetables or meats.
Add fresh herbs (e.g., cilantro, mint) for extra flavor.

Variations:
Vegetable Pulao: Use mixed vegetables.
Chicken Pulao: Use boneless chicken.
Mutton Pulao: Use boneless lamb.
Mushroom Pulao: Use sautéed mushrooms.

Nutritional Information (approximate):

Per serving (4-6 servings):
Calories: 400-500
Protein: 15-20g
Fat: 15-20g
Carbohydrates: 60-70g
Fiber: 5-7g

Pav Bhaji

Pav Bhaji is a beloved Indian street food consisting of spicy mashed vegetables, served with buttered pav (bread).

Ingredients:

For Bhaji:
2 cups mixed vegetables (potatoes, carrots, peas, cauliflower)
1 large onion, chopped
2 cloves garlic, minced
1 tablespoon ginger paste
1 teaspoon cumin seeds
1 teaspoon coriander powder
1/2 teaspoon turmeric
1/2 teaspoon red chili powder
Salt, to taste
2 tablespoons butter
2 tablespoons lemon juice

For Pav:
6-8 pav (bread rolls)
Butter, for toasting

Instructions:

Bhaji:
1. Boil mixed vegetables until tender.

2. Heat butter in a pan.
3. Add cumin seeds, onions, garlic, and ginger paste. Cook until onions are translucent.
4. Add coriander powder, turmeric, chili powder, and salt. Mix.
5. Mash boiled vegetables and add to the pan.
6. Stir Fry for 5-7 minutes.
7. Add lemon juice and mix.

Pav:
1. Toast pav on a pan with butter.
2. Serve hot with Bhaji.

Tips:
Use fresh vegetables for best results.
Adjust chili powder to desired spiciness.
Experiment with different spices (e.g., garam masala).
Add cheese or paneer for extra flavor.

Variations:
Classic Pav Bhaji: Use mixed vegetables.
Jain Pav Bhaji: Replace onions and garlic with ginger.
Mumbai Style Pav Bhaji: Add boiled potatoes.

Nutritional Information (approximate):

Per serving (4-6 servings):
Calories: 400-500
Protein: 10-12g
Fat: 20-25g
Carbohydrates: 50-60g
Fiber: 5-7g

Pav Bhaji Masala Recipe:

Mix together:
2 tablespoons coriander seeds
1 tablespoon cumin seeds
1 tablespoon cinnamon powder
1/2 tablespoon cardamom powder
1/2 tablespoon nutmeg powder
1/4 teaspoon cayenne pepper

Grind into a fine powder and store in an airtight container. Use 1-2 teaspoons in Pav Bhaji recipe.

Matar Kachori

Matar Kachori is a popular Indian snack consisting of crispy fried bread filled with spiced green peas (matar) and onions.

Ingredients:

For Dough:
2 cups all purpose flour
1 teaspoon salt
1/4 teaspoon baking powder
1/4 cup ghee or oil
1/2 cup lukewarm water

For Filling:
1 cup green peas (matar)
1/2 cup chopped onions
1/4 cup chopped cilantro
1/4 cup grated ginger
1/4 cup lemon juice
1/2 teaspoon cumin seeds
1/2 teaspoon coriander powder
1/4 teaspoon garam masala
Salt, to taste

Instructions:

Dough:

1. Mix flour, salt, and baking powder.
2. Add ghee or oil and mix.
3. Gradually add lukewarm water and knead.
4. Rest dough for 30 minutes.

Filling:
1. Heat oil in a pan.
2. Add cumin seeds and let them sizzle.
3. Add onions, peas, ginger, cilantro, lemon juice, coriander powder, garam masala, and salt. Cook until onions are translucent.

Assembly:
1. Divide dough into small balls.
2. Roll out each ball into a circle.
3. Place filling in the center.
4. Fold and seal kachori.
5. Fry until golden brown.

Tips:
Use fresh peas for best results.
Adjust spice level to desired taste.
Experiment with different fillings (e.g., potatoes, cauliflower).
Use a flavorful oil (e.g., ghee, mustard oil).

Variations:
Classic Matar Kachori: Use green peas.
Spicy Matar Kachori: Add more chili powder.
Vegan Matar Kachori: Replace ghee with oil.

Nutritional Information (approximate):

Per serving (4-6 kachoris):
Calories: 300-400
Protein: 10-12g
Fat: 15-20g
Carbohydrates: 40-50g
Fiber: 5-7g

Aloo Kulcha

Aloo Kulcha is a beloved Indian flatbread originating from North India, especially Punjab. It's a leavened, buttery flatbread stuffed with spiced potatoes (aloo) and herbs.

Ingredients:

For Dough:
2 cups all purpose flour
1 teaspoon salt
1/4 teaspoon baking powder
1/4 cup yogurt
1/4 cup lukewarm water
2 tablespoons ghee or oil

For Filling:
2 large boiled and mashed potatoes
1/4 cup chopped onions
1/4 cup chopped cilantro
1/4 cup grated ginger
1/2 teaspoon cumin seeds
1/2 teaspoon coriander powder
1/4 teaspoon garam masala
Salt, to taste
1 tablespoon lemon juice

Instructions:

Dough:
1. Mix flour, salt, and baking powder.
2. Add yogurt, lukewarm water, and ghee or oil. Mix.
3. Knead for 5-7 minutes.
4. Rest dough for 1 hour.

Filling:
1. Heat oil in a pan.
2. Add cumin seeds and let them sizzle.
3. Add onions, ginger, coriander powder, garam masala, and salt. Cook until onions are translucent.
4. Mix in mashed potatoes, cilantro, and lemon juice.

Assembly:
1. Divide dough into small balls.
2. Roll out each ball into a circle.
3. Place filling in the center.
4. Fold and seal kulcha.
5. Bake in the oven at 400°F (200°C) for 10-12 minutes or cook on tawa.

Tips:
Use fresh potatoes for best results.
Adjust spice level to desired taste.
Experiment with different fillings (e.g., cauliflower, paneer).
Use a flavorful oil (e.g., ghee, mustard oil).

Variations:
Classic Aloo Kulcha: Use potatoes.
Spicy Aloo Kulcha: Add more chili powder.
Vegan Aloo Kulcha: Replace ghee with oil.

Nutritional Information (approximate):

Per serving (4-6 kulchas):
Calories: 250-300
Protein: 5-7g
Fat: 10-12g
Carbohydrates: 35-40g
Fiber: 4-5g

Misal Pav

Misal Pav is a beloved Indian street food originating from Maharashtra, especially Mumbai and Pune. It's a spicy curry made with sprouted lentils (misal) and served with pav (bread).

Ingredients:

For Misal:
1 cup sprouted lentils (matki or moth beans)
2 cups water
1 tablespoon oil
1 onion, chopped
2 cloves garlic, minced
1 teaspoon ginger paste
1 teaspoon cumin seeds
1 teaspoon coriander powder
1/2 teaspoon turmeric
1/2 teaspoon red chili powder
Salt, to taste
2 tablespoons tamarind paste
2 tablespoons jaggery

For Pav:
6-8 pav (bread rolls)
Butter, for toasting

For Toppings:

Chopped onions
Chopped cilantro
Farsan (crunchy snack)
Lemon wedges

Instructions:

Misal:
1. Boil sprouted lentils until tender.
2. Heat oil in a pan.
3. Add cumin seeds, onions, garlic, and ginger paste. Cook until onions are translucent.
4. Add coriander powder, turmeric, chili powder, and salt. Mix.
5. Add boiled lentils, tamarind paste, and jaggery. Simmer.
6. Add water to achieve desired consistency.

Pav:
1. Toast pav on a pan with butter.

Assembly:
1. Serve Misal in a bowl.
2. Add toppings (onions, cilantro, farsan, lemon wedges).
3. Serve with toasted pav.

Tips:
Use fresh sprouted lentils for best results.
Adjust chili powder to desired spiciness.
Experiment with different toppings (e.g., cheese, sev).
Use a flavorful oil (e.g., ghee, mustard oil).

Variations:

Classic Misal Pav: Use sprouted lentils.
Spicy Misal Pav: Add more chili powder.
Vegan Misal Pav: Replace ghee with oil.

Nutritional Information (approximate):

Per serving (4-6 servings):
Calories: 400-500
Protein: 15-20g
Fat: 20-25g
Carbohydrates: 50-60g
Fiber: 5-7g

Aloo Tikki

Aloo Tikki is a beloved Indian street food consisting of crispy potato patties filled with spiced potatoes, peas, and herbs.

Ingredients:

For Aloo Mixture:
4-5 large boiled and mashed potatoes
1/2 cup peas
1/4 cup chopped onions
1/4 cup chopped cilantro
1/4 cup grated ginger
1/2 teaspoon cumin seeds
1/2 teaspoon coriander powder
1/4 teaspoon garam masala
Salt, to taste
1 tablespoon lemon juice

For Coating:
1 cup breadcrumbs
1/4 cup cornstarch
1/4 cup all purpose flour
1/4 teaspoon salt

For Frying:
Oil, for frying

Instructions:

Aloo Mixture:
1. Heat oil in a pan.
2. Add cumin seeds and let them sizzle.
3. Add onions, ginger, peas, coriander powder, garam masala, and salt.
Cook until onions are translucent.
4. Mix in mashed potatoes, cilantro, and lemon juice.

Coating:
Mix breadcrumbs, cornstarch, flour, and salt.

Assembly:
1. Divide Aloo mixture into small portions.
2. Shape into patties.
3. Coat with breadcrumb mixture.
4. Fry until golden brown.

Tips:
Use fresh potatoes for best results.
Adjust spice level to desired taste.
Experiment with different fillings (e.g., cauliflower, paneer).
Use a flavorful oil (e.g., ghee, mustard oil).

Variations:
Classic Aloo Tikki: Use potatoes and peas.
Spicy Aloo Tikki: Add more chili powder.
Vegan Aloo Tikki: Replace ghee with oil.

Nutritional Information (approximate):

Per serving (4-6 tikkis):
Calories: 250-300
Protein: 5-7g
Fat: 10-12g
Carbohydrates: 35-40g
Fiber: 4-5g

Ragda

Ragda is a beloved Indian street food consisting of spicy white pea curry served with crispy pav (bread) or crackers.

Ingredients:

For Ragda:
1 cup dried white peas (safed matar)
4 cups water
1 tablespoon oil
1 onion, chopped
2 cloves garlic, minced
1 teaspoon ginger paste
1 teaspoon cumin seeds
1 teaspoon coriander powder
1/2 teaspoon turmeric
1/2 teaspoon red chili powder
Salt, to taste
2 tablespoons tamarind paste
2 tablespoons lemon juice

For Toppings:
Chopped onions
Chopped cilantro
Sev (crunchy snack)
Lemon wedges

Instructions:

Ragda:
1. Soak white peas overnight.
2. Boil peas until tender.
3. Heat oil in a pan.
4. Add cumin seeds, onions, garlic, and ginger paste. Cook until onions are translucent.
5. Add coriander powder, turmeric, chili powder, and salt. Mix.
6. Add boiled peas, tamarind paste, and lemon juice. Simmer.
7. Adjust consistency by adding water.

Assembly:
1. Serve Ragda in a bowl.
2. Add toppings (onions, cilantro, sev, lemon wedges).
3. Serve with pav or crackers.

Tips:
Use fresh peas for best results.
Adjust chili powder to desired spiciness.
Experiment with different spices (e.g., garam masala).
Use a flavorful oil (e.g., ghee, mustard oil).

Variations:
Classic Ragda: Use white peas.
Spicy Ragda: Add more chili powder.
Vegan Ragda: Replace ghee with oil.

Nutritional Information (approximate):

Per serving (4-6 servings):

Calories: 300-400
Protein: 15-20g
Fat: 10-12g
Carbohydrates: 40-50g
Fiber: 5-7g

Ragda Patties Recipe:

Mix Ragda with boiled potatoes, onions, and breadcrumbs. Shape into patties. Coat with breadcrumb mixture. Fry until crispy. Serve with pav or crackers.

Ragda Chaat Recipe:

Mix Ragda with yogurt, tamarind chutney, and sev. Serve with pav or crackers.

Dosa

Dosa is a popular South Indian breakfast dish made from fermented rice and lentil batter, cooked into a crispy and savory crepe.

Ingredients:

For Batter:
2 cups rice
1 cup split black gram (urad dal)
1/2 cup fenugreek seeds (methi seeds)
1/4 teaspoon salt
4 cups water
1 tablespoon oil

For Filling (optional):
Potato masala (see below)
Onion, tomato, and chutney

Instructions:

Batter Preparation:
1. Rinse rice, urad dal, and methi seeds.
2. Soak for 4-5 hours.
3. Grind into a smooth paste.
4. Ferment overnight (8-10 hours).
5. Add salt and mix.

Dosa Making:
1. Heat a nonstick pan or dosa tawa.
2. Pour 1/4 cup batter.
3. Spread evenly.
4. Cook until the bottom is golden brown.
5. Flip and cook for another minute.

Potato Masala Filling:
2 large boiled potatoes, mashed
1 onion, chopped
1 tomato, chopped
1 teaspoon mustard seeds
1 teaspoon cumin seeds
Salt, to taste
2 tablespoons oil

Assembly:
1. Spread potato masala filling on dosa.
2. Fold dosa in half.
3. Serve with sambar and chutney.

Tips:
Use short grain rice for best results.
Adjust fermentation time according to climate.
Experiment with different fillings (e.g., vegetable, chicken).
Use a nonstick pan or dosa tawa.

Variations:
Classic Dosa: Use rice and urad dal.
Rava Dosa: Use semolina instead of rice.
Paper Dosa: Use less batter for a thinner dosa.
Neer Dosa: Use coconut water for fermentation.

Nutritional Information (approximate):

Per serving (4-6 dosas):
Calories: 200-300
Protein: 5-7g
Fat: 10-12g
Carbohydrates: 30-40g
Fiber: 4-5g

Vada Pav

Vada Pav is a beloved Indian street food consisting of crispy fried doughnut like dumplings (vada) served in a bread bun (pav) with chutneys and spices.

Ingredients:

For Vada:
1 cup split black gram (urad dal)
1/2 cup split Bengal gram (chana dal)
1/4 cup grated ginger
1/4 cup chopped green chilies
1/4 cup chopped cilantro
1/2 teaspoon cumin seeds
1/2 teaspoon coriander powder
Salt, to taste
1/4 teaspoon baking soda
Oil, for frying

For Pav:
6-8 pav (bread rolls)
Butter, for toasting

For Chutneys:
Green chutney (see below)
Tamarind chutney (see below)
Garlic chutney (see below)

Instructions:

Vada Preparation:
1. Soak urad dal and chana dal for 4-5 hours.
2. Grind into a coarse paste.
3. Add ginger, green chilies, cilantro, cumin seeds, coriander powder, salt, and baking soda. Mix.
4. Shape into small dumplings.
5. Fry until golden brown.

Pav Toasting:
Toast pav on a pan with butter.

Assembly:
1. Place vada in pav.
2. Add green chutney, tamarind chutney, and garlic chutney.
3. Serve immediately.

Chutney Recipes:
Green Chutney: Blend cilantro, green chilies, ginger, garlic, and lemon juice.
Tamarind Chutney: Cook tamarind paste, jaggery, and spices.
Garlic Chutney: Blend garlic, red chilies, and vinegar.

Tips:
Use fresh dal for best results.
Adjust spice level to desired taste.
Experiment with different chutneys.
Use a flavorful oil (e.g., ghee, mustard oil).

Variations:
Classic Vada Pav: Use urad dal and chana dal.
Spicy Vada Pav: Add more green chilies.
Vegan Vada Pav: Replace ghee with oil.

Nutritional Information (approximate):

Per serving (4-6 vada pav):
Calories: 400-500
Protein: 15-20g
Fat: 20-25g
Carbohydrates: 50-60g
Fiber: 5-7g

Matar Kulcha

Matar Kulcha is a beloved Indian flatbread originating from North India, especially Punjab. It's a leavened, buttery flatbread stuffed with spiced green peas (matar) and herbs.

Ingredients:

For Dough:
2 cups all purpose flour
1 teaspoon salt
1/4 teaspoon baking powder
1/4 cup yogurt
1/4 cup lukewarm water
2 tablespoons ghee or oil

For Filling:
1 cup green peas (matar)
1/4 cup chopped onions
1/4 cup chopped cilantro
1/4 cup grated ginger
1/2 teaspoon cumin seeds
1/2 teaspoon coriander powder
1/4 teaspoon garam masala
Salt, to taste
1 tablespoon lemon juice

Instructions:

Dough Preparation:
1. Mix flour, salt, and baking powder.
2. Add yogurt, lukewarm water, and ghee or oil. Mix.
3. Knead for 5-7 minutes.
4. Rest dough for 1 hour.

Filling Preparation:
1. Heat oil in a pan.
2. Add cumin seeds and let them sizzle.
3. Add onions, ginger, peas, coriander powder, garam masala, and salt. Cook until onions are translucent.
4. Mix in cilantro and lemon juice.

Assembly:
1. Divide dough into small balls.
2. Roll out each ball into a circle.
3. Place filling in the center.
4. Fold and seal kulcha.
5. Bake in the oven at 400°F (200°C) for 10-12 minutes or cook on tawa.

Tips:
Use fresh peas for best results.
Adjust spice level to desired taste.
Experiment with different fillings (e.g., cauliflower, paneer).
Use a flavorful oil (e.g., ghee, mustard oil).

Variations:
Classic Matar Kulcha: Use green peas.
Spicy Matar Kulcha: Add more chili powder.
Vegan Matar Kulcha: Replace ghee with oil.

Nutritional Information (approximate):

Per serving (4-6 kulchas):
Calories: 250-300
Protein: 5-7g
Fat: 10-12g
Carbohydrates: 35-40g
Fiber: 4-5g

Papdi Chaat

Papdi Chaat is a beloved Indian street food consisting of crispy fried bread (papdi) topped with yogurt, chutneys, potatoes, onions, and chickpeas.

Ingredients:

For Papdi:
2 cups all purpose flour
1/2 cup semolina
1/4 teaspoon salt
1/4 teaspoon baking powder
1/4 cup ghee or oil
1/2 cup lukewarm water

For Chaat:
1 cup yogurt
1/2 cup tamarind chutney
1/2 cup green chutney
1/2 cup chickpeas
1/2 cup diced potatoes
1/4 cup diced onions
1/4 cup chopped cilantro
Salt, to taste
Chaat masala, to taste

Instructions:

Papdi Preparation:
1. Mix flour, semolina, salt, and baking powder.
2. Add ghee or oil and mix.
3. Gradually add lukewarm water and knead.
4. Rest dough for 30 minutes.
5. Roll out dough into thin circles.
6. Fry until crispy.

Chaat Assembly:
1. Arrange papdi on a plate.
2. Top with yogurt, tamarind chutney, green chutney, chickpeas, potatoes, onions, and cilantro.
3. Sprinkle salt and chaat masala.
4. Serve immediately.

Tips:
Use fresh ingredients for best results.
Adjust chutney quantities to desired taste.
Experiment with different toppings (e.g., paneer, sev).
Use a flavorful oil (e.g., ghee, mustard oil).

Variations:
Classic Papdi Chaat: Use yogurt and chutneys.
Spicy Papdi Chaat: Add more chili powder.
Vegan Papdi Chaat: Replace ghee with oil.

Nutritional Information (approximate):

Per serving (4-6 servings):
Calories: 300-400

Protein: 10-12g
Fat: 15-20g
Carbohydrates: 40-50g
Fiber: 5-7g

Chutney Recipes:
Tamarind Chutney: Cook tamarind paste, jaggery, and spices.
Green Chutney: Blend cilantro, green chilies, ginger, garlic, and lemon juice.

Chaat Masala Recipe:

Mix together:
2 tablespoons coriander powder
1 tablespoon cumin powder
1 tablespoon garam masala
1 tablespoon amchur powder
1/2 tablespoon cayenne pepper
Salt, to taste

Puri Bhaji

Puri Bhaji is a beloved Indian breakfast dish consisting of deep fried puffed bread (puri) served with a spicy potato based curry (bhaji).

Ingredients:

For Puri:
2 cups all purpose flour
1/4 teaspoon salt
1/4 teaspoon baking powder
1/4 cup ghee or oil
1/2 cup lukewarm water

For Bhaji:
2 large boiled and mashed potatoes
1 onion, chopped
2 cloves garlic, minced
1 teaspoon cumin seeds
1 teaspoon coriander powder
1/2 teaspoon turmeric
1/2 teaspoon red chili powder
Salt, to taste
2 tablespoons lemon juice
2 tablespoons chopped cilantro

Instructions:

Puri Preparation:

1. Mix flour, salt, and baking powder.
2. Add ghee or oil and mix.
3. Gradually add lukewarm water and knead.
4. Rest dough for 30 minutes.
5. Divide into small balls.
6. Roll out each ball into a circle.
7. Fry until puffed and golden.

Bhaji Preparation:

1. Heat oil in a pan.
2. Add cumin seeds and let them sizzle.
3. Add onions, garlic, coriander powder, turmeric, chili powder, and salt. Cook until onions are translucent.
4. Mix in mashed potatoes, lemon juice, and cilantro.

Assembly:

1. Serve puri with bhaji.
2. Garnish with chopped cilantro and lemon wedges.

Tips:

Use fresh potatoes for best results.
Adjust chili powder to desired spiciness.
Experiment with different spices (e.g., garam masala).
Use a flavorful oil (e.g., ghee, mustard oil).

Variations:

Classic Puri Bhaji: Use potatoes and onions.
Spicy Puri Bhaji: Add more chili powder.
Vegan Puri Bhaji: Replace ghee with oil.

Nutritional Information (approximate):

Per serving (4-6 servings):
Calories: 400-500
Protein: 10-12g
Fat: 20-25g
Carbohydrates: 50-60g
Fiber: 5-7g

Koraishutir Kochuri

Koraishutir Kochuri is a classic Bengali flatbread filled with a spicy pea filling, typically served during winter months.

Ingredients:

For Dough:
2 cups all purpose flour
1/4 teaspoon salt
1/4 teaspoon baking powder
1/4 cup ghee or oil
1/2 cup lukewarm water

For Filling:
1 cup fresh or frozen peas
1/2 cup chopped onions
1/4 cup chopped cilantro
1/4 cup grated ginger
1/2 teaspoon cumin seeds
1/2 teaspoon coriander powder
1/4 teaspoon turmeric
1/4 teaspoon red chili powder
Salt, to taste
1 tablespoon lemon juice

Instructions:

Dough Preparation:
1. Mix flour, salt, and baking powder.
2. Add ghee or oil and mix.
3. Gradually add lukewarm water and knead.
4. Rest dough for 30 minutes.

Filling Preparation:
1. Heat oil in a pan.
2. Add cumin seeds and let them sizzle.
3. Add onions, ginger, peas, coriander powder, turmeric, chili powder, and salt. Cook until onions are translucent.
4. Mix in cilantro and lemon juice.

Assembly:
1. Divide dough into small balls.
2. Roll out each ball into a circle.
3. Place filling in the center.
4. Fold and seal kochuri.
5. Fry until golden brown or bake in the oven.

Tips:
Use fresh peas for best results.
Adjust chili powder to desired spiciness.
Experiment with different fillings (e.g., cauliflower, potato).
Use a flavorful oil (e.g., ghee, mustard oil).

Variations:
Classic Koraishutir Kochuri: Use peas and onions.
Spicy Koraishutir Kochuri: Add more chili powder.
Vegan Koraishutir Kochuri: Replace ghee with oil.

Nutritional Information (approximate):

Per serving (4-6 kochuris):
Calories: 300-400
Protein: 10-12g
Fat: 15-20g
Carbohydrates: 40-50g
Fiber: 5-7g

Masala Puri

Masala Puri is a popular Indian street food snack consisting of crispy, flavorful puris (fried bread) seasoned with a spicy masala blend.

Ingredients:

For Puri:
2 cups all purpose flour
1/4 teaspoon salt
1/4 teaspoon baking powder
1/4 cup ghee or oil
1/2 cup lukewarm water

For Masala:
2 tablespoons coriander seeds
1 tablespoon cumin seeds
1 tablespoon fennel seeds
1 tablespoon garam masala
1 tablespoon amchur powder
1/2 teaspoon red chili powder
Salt, to taste

Instructions:

Puri Preparation:
1. Mix flour, salt, and baking powder.
2. Add ghee or oil and mix.

3. Gradually add lukewarm water and knead.
4. Rest dough for 30 minutes.
5. Divide into small balls.
6. Roll out each ball into a circle.
7. Fry until golden brown.

Masala Preparation:
1. Dry roast coriander seeds, cumin seeds, and fennel seeds.
2. Grind into a fine powder.
3. Mix with garam masala, amchur powder, chili powder, and salt.

Assembly:
1. Fry puris until crispy.
2. Sprinkle masala blend over puris.
3. Serve immediately.

Tips:
Use fresh spices for best results.
Adjust chili powder to desired spiciness.
Experiment with different masala blends.
Use a flavorful oil (e.g., ghee, mustard oil).

Variations:
Classic Masala Puri: Use coriander seeds and cumin seeds.
Spicy Masala Puri: Add more chili powder.
Vegan Masala Puri: Replace ghee with oil.

Nutritional Information (approximate):

Per serving (4-6 puris):
Calories: 250-300

Protein: 5-7g
Fat: 10-12g
Carbohydrates: 35-40g
Fiber: 4-5g

Paneer Tikka

Paneer Tikka is a beloved Indian appetizer consisting of marinated paneer (Indian cheese) grilled to perfection.

Ingredients:

For Marinade:
250g paneer, cut into cubes
1/2 cup yogurt
2 tablespoons lemon juice
2 tablespoons ghee or oil
2 teaspoons garam masala
1 teaspoon cumin powder
1 teaspoon coriander powder
1/2 teaspoon cayenne pepper (optional)
Salt, to taste
Chopped cilantro, for garnish

For Grill:
Skewers or grill pan

Instructions:

Marinade Preparation:
1. Mix yogurt, lemon juice, ghee or oil, garam masala, cumin powder, coriander powder, cayenne pepper (if using), and salt.
2. Add paneer cubes and mix well.

3. Refrigerate for 30 minutes to 2 hours.

Grilling:
1. Preheat the grill or grill pan.
2. Thread marinated paneer onto skewers.
3. Grill until golden brown and slightly charred.
4. Brush with butter or ghee.

Assembly:
1. Serve Paneer Tikka hot.
2. Garnish with chopped cilantro.
3. Accompany with chutney or raita.

Tips:
Use fresh paneer for best results.
Adjust marinade time for desired flavor.
Experiment with different spice blends.
Use a flavorful oil (e.g., ghee, mustard oil).

Variations:
Classic Paneer Tikka: Use yogurt and lemon juice.
Spicy Paneer Tikka: Add more cayenne pepper.
Vegan Paneer Tikka: Replace paneer with tofu.

Nutritional Information (approximate):

Per serving (4-6 servings):
Calories: 200-250
Protein: 15-20g
Fat: 10-12g
Carbohydrates: 10-12g

Fiber: 2-3g

76 HENRY ZOTHANMAWIA

Fiber: 2-3g

Dhokla

Dhokla is a beloved Gujarati snack made from fermented rice and lentil batter, steamed to perfection.

Ingredients:

For Batter:
1 cup rice
1/2 cup split black gram (urad dal)
1/4 cup yogurt
1/4 teaspoon salt
1/4 teaspoon baking soda
1 tablespoon oil
1 tablespoon lemon juice
Chopped cilantro, for garnish

For Tempering:
1 tablespoon oil
1 teaspoon mustard seeds
1 teaspoon cumin seeds
1/4 teaspoon asafoetida (hing)
1/4 teaspoon turmeric

Instructions:

Batter Preparation:
1. Soak rice and urad dal for 4-5 hours.

2. Grind into a smooth paste.

3. Mix yogurt, salt, baking soda, oil, and lemon juice.

4. Ferment for 8-10 hours.

Tempering Preparation:

1. Heat oil in a pan.

2. Add mustard seeds, cumin seeds, asafoetida, and turmeric.

3. Let seeds sizzle.

Assembly:

1. Grease a steamer plate.

2. Pour batter onto a plate.

3. Add tempering mixture.

4. Steam for 15-20 minutes.

5. Cut into squares.

Tips:

Use short grain rice for best results.

Adjust fermentation time according to climate.

Experiment with different seasonings.

Use a flavorful oil (e.g., ghee, mustard oil).

Variations:

Classic Dhokla: Use rice and urad dal.

Spicy Dhokla: Add more chili powder.

Vegan Dhokla: Replace yogurt with a non dairy alternative.

Nutritional Information (approximate):

Per serving (4-6 servings):

Calories: 200-250

Protein: 5-7g
Fat: 10-12g
Carbohydrates: 30-35g
Fiber: 4-5g

Thali

Thali is a classic Indian meal consisting of a variety of dishes served together on a platter.

Thali Components:
1. Rice (Chawal)
2. Roti/Chapati (Flatbread)
3. Dal (Lentil Curry)
4. Vegetable Sabzi (StirFried Vegetables)
5. Raita (Yogurt Side Dish)
6. Papadum (Thin Flatbread)
7. Chutney (Spicy Condiment)
8. Salad (Optional)

Recipes:

Rice (Chawal)
1 cup basmati rice
2 cups water
Salt, to taste

Roti/Chapati
2 cups whole wheat flour
1/2 cup lukewarm water
Salt, to taste

Dal

1 cup split red lentils
2 cups water
1 onion, chopped
1 tomato, chopped
1 teaspoon cumin seeds
Salt, to taste

Vegetable Sabzi
1 cup mixed vegetables (e.g., cauliflower, carrots, peas)
1 onion, chopped
1 tomato, chopped
1 teaspoon cumin seeds
Salt, to taste

Raita
1 cup yogurt
1/2 cup chopped cucumber
1/4 cup chopped cilantro
Salt, to taste

Papadum
1 cup papadum
Oil, for frying

Chutney
1 cup chopped cilantro
1/2 cup green chilies
1/4 cup lemon juice
Salt, to taste

Instructions:

1. Prepare each component separately.
2. Arrange components on a thali platter.
3. Serve hot.

Tips:
Use fresh ingredients for best results.
Adjust spice levels to desired taste.
Experiment with different regional variations.
Use a flavorful oil (e.g., ghee, mustard oil).

Nutritional Information (approximate):

Per serving (4-6 servings):
Calories: 800-1000
Protein: 20-25g
Fat: 20-25g
Carbohydrates: 100-120g
Fiber: 10-12g

Papadum

Papadum is a thin, crisp Indian flatbread typically served as an accompaniment to meals.

Ingredients:
2 cups lentil flour (urad dal or moong dal)
1/2 cup water
1/4 teaspoon salt
1/4 teaspoon baking soda
1 tablespoon ghee or oil
Optional: spices (e.g., cumin seeds, coriander powder)

Instructions:

Dough Preparation:
1. Mix flour, salt, and baking soda.
2. Gradually add water and knead.
3. Rest dough for 30 minutes.

Rolling:
1. Divide dough into small balls.
2. Roll out each ball into a thin circle (7-8 inches diameter).

Frying:
1. Heat oil in a deep frying pan.
2. Fry papadum until crispy and golden.
3. Drain excess oil.

Roasting:
1. Preheat the oven to 400°F (200°C).
2. Place papadum on a baking sheet.
3. Roast for 5-7 minutes or until crispy.

Microwaving:
1. Place papadum on a microwave safe plate.
2. Cook for 30-45 seconds or until crispy.

Tips:
Use lentil flour for authentic flavor.
Adjust water for desired dough consistency.
Experiment with spices for unique flavors.
Use a flavorful oil (e.g., ghee, mustard oil).

Variations:
Classic Papadum: Use urad dal flour.
Spicy Papadum: Add red chili powder.
Garlic Papadum: Mix in minced garlic.

Nutritional Information (approximate):

Per serving (4-6 papadum):
Calories: 150-200
Protein: 5-7g
Fat: 5-7g
Carbohydrates: 25-30g
Fiber: 4-5g

Bhutta

Bhutta is a popular Indian street food, especially during monsoons, made by grilling corn on the cob over an open flame.

Ingredients:
4-6 corn on the cob
2 tablespoons butter or ghee
1 teaspoon lemon juice
1 teaspoon chili powder
1 teaspoon garam masala
Salt, to taste
Chopped cilantro, for garnish

Instructions:
1. Preheat the grill or grill pan.
2. Brush corn with butter or ghee.
3. Sprinkle lemon juice, chili powder, garam masala, and salt.
4. Grill corn for 10-12 minutes, turning frequently.
5. Char slightly for smoky flavor.
6. Garnish with cilantro.

Tips:
Use fresh corn for best results.
Adjust spice level to desired taste.
Experiment with different seasonings (e.g., garlic, herbs).
Grill over medium heat for even cooking.

Variations:

Classic Bhutta: Use butter and chili powder.

Spicy Bhutta: Add more chili powder.

Herby Bhutta: Mix in chopped herbs (e.g., parsley, basil).

Nutritional Information (approximate):

Per serving (4-6 servings):

Calories: 150-200

Protein: 3-4g

Fat: 2-3g

Carbohydrates: 30-35g

Fiber: 4-5g

Lassi

Lassi is a popular Indian beverage made with yogurt, water, and spices, perfect for hot summer days.

Ingredients:
1 cup yogurt (dahi)
1/2 cup water
1/4 teaspoon salt
1/4 teaspoon cardamom powder (elaichi)
1/4 teaspoon cumin powder (jeera)
1 tablespoon sugar (optional)
Ice cubes (optional)
Chopped cilantro or mint for garnish

Instructions:
1. In a blender, combine yogurt, water, salt, cardamom powder, and cumin powder.
2. Blend until smooth and creamy.
3. Add sugar, if desired, and blend well.
4. Taste and adjust sweetness or spice level.
5. Pour into glasses and serve chilled.
6. Garnish with chopped cilantro or mint.

Variations:
Sweet Lassi: Add more sugar or honey to taste.
Salty Lassi: Increase salt to 1/2 teaspoon.
Spicy Lassi: Add a pinch of cayenne pepper or red chili powder.

Fruit Lassi: Blend in pureed fruit (e.g., mango, banana, strawberry).
Herbal Lassi: Infuse with herbs like mint, basil, or lemongrass.

Tips:
Use fresh yogurt for best results.
Adjust water ratio to desired consistency.
Experiment with different spices or flavorings.
Serve chilled, with ice cubes if desired.

Nutritional Information (approximate):

Per serving (4-6 servings):
Calories: 100-150
Protein: 10-12g
Fat: 5-7g
Carbohydrates: 15-20g
Fiber: 2-3g

Health Benefits:
High in protein and calcium
Supports digestive health
Refreshing and hydrating
Can aid in weight management

Regional Variations:
Punjabi Lassi: Thicker and creamier, with more sugar.
Rajasthani Lassi: Thinner and more spicy.
South Indian Lassi: With coconut milk or fruit puree.

Falooda

Falooda is a beloved Indian dessert drink made with vermicelli noodles, milk, sugar, and rose syrup, topped with fruits and nuts.

Ingredients:
1 cup vermicelli noodles
2 cups milk
1 cup sugar
1/4 cup rose syrup
1/4 cup chopped pistachios
1/4 cup chopped almonds
1 scoop vanilla ice cream
Fruits (e.g., strawberries, blueberries, banana)
Whipped cream (optional)

Instructions:
1. Cook vermicelli noodles according to package instructions.
2. In a saucepan, combine milk, sugar, and rose syrup.
3. Heat until sugar dissolves.
4. Chill the mixture in the refrigerator.
5. Assemble Falooda by layering:
Vermicelli noodles
Milk mixture
Fruits
Nuts
Ice cream
Whipped cream (if using)

Tips:
Use thin vermicelli noodles for best results.
Adjust rose syrup to desired sweetness.
Experiment with different fruits and nuts.
Serve chilled and immediately.

Variations:
Kesar Falooda: Add saffron threads to the milk mixture.
Pistachio Falooda: Use pistachio syrup instead of rose.
Fruit Falooda: Add more fruits and less nuts.
Dry Fruit Falooda: Use dry fruits like dates and apricots.

Nutritional Information (approximate):

Per serving (4-6 servings):
Calories: 300-400
Protein: 10-12g
Fat: 15-20g
Carbohydrates: 40-50g
Fiber: 4-5g

Health Benefits:
Rich in calcium and protein
Good source of fiber
Can aid in digestion
Refreshing and cooling

Regional Variations:

Mumbai Style Falooda: Thicker and creamier.

Delhi Style Falooda: More rose syrup and nuts.
Kolkata Style Falooda: With mishti doi (sweet curd).

Kheer

Kheer is a beloved Indian dessert made with rice, milk, sugar, and spices, often served at special occasions.

Ingredients:
1 cup basmati rice
4 cups milk
1 cup sugar
1/4 teaspoon cardamom powder (elaichi)
1/4 teaspoon saffron threads (optional)
1/4 teaspoon nutmeg powder (jaiphal)
2 tablespoons ghee or unsalted butter
Chopped nuts (e.g., almonds, pistachios) for garnish

Instructions:
1. Rinse rice and soak in water for 30 minutes.
2. Drain and cook rice in milk, stirring constantly.
3. Add sugar, cardamom powder, saffron threads (if using), and nutmeg powder.
4. Cook until rice is tender and mixture thickens.
5. Add ghee or butter and stir well.
6. Simmer for 5-7 minutes or until desired consistency.
7. Garnish with chopped nuts.

Tips:
Use short grain rice for a creamy texture.
Adjust sugar to desired sweetness.

Experiment with spices (e.g., cinnamon, cloves).
Serve chilled or warm.

Variations:
Saffron Kheer: Add more saffron threads for vibrant color.
Dry Fruit Kheer: Add chopped dry fruits (e.g., dates, apricots).
Fruit Kheer: Mix in pureed fruits (e.g., mango, banana).
Vegan Kheer: Replace milk with plant based milk and ghee with oil.

Nutritional Information (approximate):

Per serving (4-6 servings):
Calories: 250-300
Protein: 5-7g
Fat: 10-12g
Carbohydrates: 40-50g
Fiber: 2-3g

Health Benefits:
Rich in carbohydrates for energy
Good source of calcium and protein
Can aid in digestion
Comforting and soothing dessert

Regional Variations:
North Indian Kheer: Thicker and creamier.
South Indian Payasam: Thinner and sweeter.
Bengali Kheer: With mustard oil and dried fruits.

Malpua

Malpua is a popular Indian dessert made with deep fried batter balls, soaked in syrup, and often served during festivals.

Ingredients:

For Batter:
1 cup all purpose flour
1/2 cup milk powder
1/4 teaspoon baking powder
1/4 teaspoon cardamom powder (elaichi)
1/4 teaspoon saffron threads (optional)
1/2 cup lukewarm milk
1/4 cup ghee or oil
Chopped nuts (e.g., almonds, pistachios) for garnish

For Syrup:
1 cup sugar
1 cup water
1/4 teaspoon cardamom powder (elaichi)
1/4 teaspoon rose water (optional)

Instructions:

Batter Preparation:
1. Mix flour, milk powder, baking powder, cardamom powder, and saffron threads (if using).

2. Gradually add lukewarm milk and ghee or oil.

3. Knead smooth batter.

Frying Malpua:

1. Heat oil in a deep frying pan.

2. Using a spoon, drop small batter balls into oil.

3. Fry until golden brown.

4. Drain excess oil.

Syrup Preparation:

1. Combine sugar, water, cardamom powder, and rose water (if using).

2. Heat until sugar dissolves.

3. Simmer until syrup thickens.

Assembly:

1. Soak fried malpua in syrup for 5-7 minutes.

2. Garnish with chopped nuts.

3. Serve warm or chilled.

Tips:

Use lukewarm milk for smooth batter.

Adjust syrup consistency to desired thickness.

Experiment with spices (e.g., cinnamon, cloves).

Serve with rabri or kulfi for added flavor.

Variations:

Rajasthani Malpua: With khoya (milk solids) and dry fruits.

Bengali Malpua: With jaggery and coconut.

Gujarati Malpua: With cardamom and saffron.

Nutritional Information (approximate):

Per serving (4-6 servings):
Calories: 300-400
Protein: 5-7g
Fat: 15-20g
Carbohydrates: 40-50g
Fiber: 2-3g

Health Benefits:
Rich in carbohydrates for energy
Good source of calcium and protein
Can aid in digestion
Comforting and soothing dessert

Regional Variations:
North Indian Malpua: Crispy exterior and soft interior.
South Indian Malpua: Softer and sweeter.
East Indian Malpua: With jaggery and coconut.

Gulab Jamun

Gulab Jamun is a beloved Indian dessert consisting of deep fried dumplings soaked in rosewater infused syrup.

Ingredients:

For Dumplings:
1 cup milk powder
1/2 cup all purpose flour
1/4 teaspoon baking powder
1/4 teaspoon salt
1/4 cup ghee or oil
1/2 cup lukewarm milk

For Syrup:
1 cup sugar
1 cup water
1/4 cup rose water
1/4 teaspoon cardamom powder (elaichi)
1/4 teaspoon saffron threads (optional)

Instructions:

Dumpling Preparation:
1. Mix milk powder, flour, baking powder, and salt.
2. Gradually add ghee or oil and lukewarm milk.
3. Knead smooth dough.

Frying Dumplings:
1. Heat oil in a deep frying pan.
2. Make small dumplings and fry until golden brown.
3. Drain excess oil.

Syrup Preparation:
1. Combine sugar, water, rose water, cardamom powder, and saffron threads (if using).
2. Heat until sugar dissolves.
3. Simmer until syrup thickens.

Assembly:
1. Soak fried dumplings in syrup for 5-7 minutes.
2. Serve warm or chilled.

Tips:
Use lukewarm milk for smooth dough.
Adjust syrup consistency to desired thickness.
Experiment with spices (e.g., cinnamon, cloves).
Serve with rabri or kulfi for added flavor.

Variations:
Rajasthani Gulab Jamun: With khoya (milk solids) and dry fruits.
Bengali Gulab Jamun: With jaggery and coconut.
Gujarati Gulab Jamun: With cardamom and saffron.

Nutritional Information (approximate):

Per serving (4-6 servings):
Calories: 300-400

Protein: 5-7g
Fat: 15-20g
Carbohydrates: 40-50g
Fiber: 2-3g

Health Benefits:
Rich in carbohydrates for energy
Good source of calcium and protein
Can aid in digestion
Comforting and soothing dessert

Regional Variations:
North Indian Gulab Jamun: Crispy exterior and soft interior.
South Indian Gulab Jamun: Softer and sweeter.
East Indian Gulab Jamun: With jaggery and coconut.

Halwa

Halwa is a popular Indian dessert made with semolina, sugar, and ghee, often served at special occasions.

Ingredients:
1 cup semolina (rava or sooji)
2 cups water
1 cup sugar
1/2 cup ghee or unsalted butter
1/4 teaspoon cardamom powder (elaichi)
1/4 teaspoon saffron threads (optional)
Chopped nuts (e.g., almonds, pistachios) for garnish

Instructions:
1. Heat ghee or butter in a pan.
2. Add semolina and roast until golden brown.
3. Add water and sugar, stirring constantly.
4. Cook until mixture thickens.
5. Add cardamom powder and saffron threads (if using).
6. Stir well and remove from heat.
7. Garnish with chopped nuts.

Tips:
Use fine semolina for a smooth texture.
Adjust sugar to desired sweetness.
Experiment with spices (e.g., cinnamon, cloves).
Serve warm or chilled.

Variations:
Suji Halwa: With semolina and no nuts.
Atta Halwa: With wheat flour instead of semolina.
Gajar Halwa: With grated carrots.
Moong Dal Halwa: With split green gram.

Nutritional Information (approximate):

Per serving (4-6 servings):
Calories: 250-300
Protein: 5-7g
Fat: 10-12g
Carbohydrates: 40-50g
Fiber: 2-3g

Health Benefits:
Rich in carbohydrates for energy
Good source of fiber and protein
Can aid in digestion
Comforting and soothing dessert

Regional Variations:
North Indian Halwa: Thicker and sweeter.
South Indian Halwa: Softer and less sweet.
East Indian Halwa: With jaggery and coconut.

Additional Tips:
Use a nonstick pan to prevent sticking.
Stir constantly to prevent burning.
Adjust consistency with water or milk.

Serve with rabri or kulfi for added flavor.

Kebab

Kebabs are a popular Indian snack made with marinated meat or vegetables, grilled to perfection.

Chicken Kebab Recipe:

Ingredients:
500g boneless chicken breast or thighs
1/2 cup plain yogurt
2 tablespoons lemon juice
2 tablespoons ghee or oil
2 teaspoons cumin powder
1 teaspoon coriander powder
1 teaspoon garam masala
1/2 teaspoon cayenne pepper (optional)
Salt, to taste
Chopped cilantro, for garnish

Instructions:
1. In a bowl, mix yogurt, lemon juice, ghee or oil, cumin powder, coriander powder, garam masala, cayenne pepper (if using), and salt.
2. Add chicken and marinate for 30 minutes to 2 hours.
3. Preheat the grill or grill pan.
4. Thread marinated chicken onto skewers.
5. Grill for 5-7 minutes per side or until cooked through.
6. Garnish with chopped cilantro.

Vegetable Kebab Variation:
Replace chicken with marinated vegetables (e.g., bell peppers, onions, mushrooms, potatoes).
Adjust spices according to vegetable choices.

Tips:
Use tender meat for best results.
Adjust marinade time for desired flavor.
Experiment with spices (e.g., cinnamon, cardamom).
Serve with chutney or raita.

Types of Kebabs:
Seekh Kebab: Minced meat kebab.
Shami Kebab: Meat patties.
Tandoori Kebab: Marinated meat cooked in a clay oven.
Reshmi Kebab: Chicken kebab with creamy sauce.

Nutritional Information (approximate):

Per serving (4-6 servings):
Calories: 200-300
Protein: 25-30g
Fat: 10-12g
Carbohydrates: 10-15g
Fiber: 2-3g

Health Benefits:
High Quality protein source
Rich in vitamins and minerals
Can aid in weight management
Supports healthy digestion

Regional Variations:

North Indian Kebab: Spicier and more flavorful.

South Indian Kebab: Milder and coconut based.

Middle Eastern Kebab: With sumac and pomegranate molasses.

Shawarma

Shawarma is a popular Middle Eastern street food made with marinated meat, served in a pita bread with vegetables and tahini sauce.

Ingredients:

For Meat:
500g lamb or chicken breast, thinly sliced
1/4 cup olive oil
2 cloves garlic, minced
1 tablespoon lemon juice
1 teaspoon cumin powder
1 teaspoon paprika
Salt and pepper, to taste

For Tahini Sauce:
1/2 cup tahini
1/4 cup lemon juice
1/4 cup water
2 cloves garlic, minced
Salt, to taste

For Assembly:
4-6 pita breads
Chopped vegetables (tomatoes, onions, cucumbers, parsley)
Pickled turnips or pickles
Sumac or paprika, for garnish

Instructions:

Meat Preparation:
1. In a bowl, mix olive oil, garlic, lemon juice, cumin powder, paprika, salt, and pepper.
2. Add sliced meat and marinate for 30 minutes to 2 hours.
3. Preheat the grill or grill pan.
4. Cook meat until browned and cooked through.

Tahini Sauce Preparation:
1. Mix tahini, lemon juice, water, garlic, and salt.
2. Adjust consistency and taste.

Assembly:
1. Warm pita bread.
2. Spread tahini sauce on each bread.
3. Add cooked meat, chopped vegetables, and pickled turnips.
4. Garnish with sumac or paprika.

Tips:
Use thinly sliced meat for easy cooking.
Adjust marinade time for desired flavor.
Experiment with spices (e.g., cinnamon, cardamom).
Serve with falafel or hummus for added flavor.

Variations:
Chicken Shawarma: Replace lamb with chicken.
Vegetarian Shawarma: Replace meat with grilled vegetables.
Turkish Doner Kebab: Use lamb and add spices.

Nutritional Information (approximate):

Per serving (4-6 servings):
Calories: 400-500
Protein: 30-40g
Fat: 20-25g
Carbohydrates: 30-40g
Fiber: 5-7g

Health Benefits:
High Quality protein source
Rich in vitamins and minerals
Can aid in weight management
Supports healthy digestion

Regional Variations:
Egyptian Shawarma: Spicier and more flavorful.
Turkish Shawarma: Thinner pita bread and more lamb.
Greek Shawarma: Add feta cheese and olives.

Banta

Banta is a popular Indian lemonade made with lemon juice, spices, and carbonated water, served in a distinctive glass bottle with a marble.

Ingredients:

1 cup freshly squeezed lemon juice
1 cup sugar
1/2 cup water
1/4 teaspoon salt
1/4 teaspoon black salt (kala namak)
1/4 teaspoon cumin powder
1/4 teaspoon mint leaves
Carbonated water (e.g., soda water)
Ice cubes
Lemon wedges and mint leaves for garnish
Marble for sealing bottle (optional)

Instructions:
1. Mix lemon juice, sugar, water, salt, black salt, cumin powder, and mint leaves.
2. Stir until sugar dissolves.
3. Chill mixture in refrigerator.
4. Fill glass bottles with ice cubes.
5. Pour chilled mixture over ice cubes.
6. Top with carbonated water.
7. Stir gently.

8. Garnish with lemon wedges and mint leaves.
9. Seal bottle with marble (if using).

Tips:
Use fresh lemons for the best flavor.
Adjust sweetness and spice level.
Experiment with spices (e.g., cinnamon, cardamom).
Serve immediately.

Variations:
Shikanji Banta: Add ginger juice and cumin powder.
Masala Banta: Add more spices (e.g., cayenne pepper, black pepper).
Fruit Banta: Mix with fruit juices (e.g., orange, grapefruit).

Nutritional Information (approximate):

Per serving (4-6 servings):
Calories: 120-150
Protein: 1-2g
Fat: 0-1g
Carbohydrates: 30-40g
Fiber: 2-3g

Health Benefits:
Rich in vitamin C
Aids digestion
Refreshing and hydrating
Can help reduce heat stroke

Regional Variations:
North Indian Banta: More spicy and salty.

South Indian Banta: Sweeter and less spicy.
East Indian Banta: With ginger and cumin.

Banta Serving Tips:
Serve in a glass bottle with a marble for authenticity.
Garnish with lemon wedges and mint leaves.
Serve immediately after preparation.
Experiment with different glass shapes and sizes.
Pair with Indian street food or snacks.

Chole Kulcha

Chole Kulcha is a beloved Indian street food originating from Punjab, consisting of spicy chickpea curry (Chole) served with crispy, flaky flatbread (Kulcha).

Chole Recipe:

Ingredients:
1 cup chickpeas (chana)
2 medium onions, chopped
2 medium tomatoes, chopped
1 teaspoon cumin seeds
1 teaspoon coriander powder
1 teaspoon garam masala
1/2 teaspoon turmeric
1/2 teaspoon red chili powder
Salt, to taste
2 tablespoons oil
2 tablespoons lemon juice
Chopped cilantro, for garnish

Instructions:
1. Soak chickpeas overnight.
2. Cook chickpeas until tender.
3. Heat oil, add cumin seeds, onions, and tomatoes.
4. Add spices, salt, and cooked chickpeas.
5. Simmer until thickened.

6. Add lemon juice.

Kulcha Recipe:

Ingredients:
2 cups all purpose flour
1/4 teaspoon salt
1/4 teaspoon sugar
1/2 teaspoon active dry yeast
1/2 cup lukewarm water
2 tablespoons ghee or oil

Instructions:
1. Mix flour, salt, sugar, and yeast.
2. Add lukewarm water, ghee or oil.
3. Knead dough.
4. Rest for 1 hour.
5. Divide into 6-8 portions.
6. Roll each portion into a ball.
7. Flatten into oval shapes.
8. Bake in an oven or cook on tawa.

Assembly:
1. Serve Chole over Kulcha.
2. Garnish with chopped cilantro.
3. Add onion, lemon wedges, and chutney (optional).

Tips:
Use fresh spices for the best flavor.
Adjust chili powder for desired heat.
Experiment with variations (e.g., adding potatoes, cauliflower).

Serve immediately.

Variations:
Amritsari Kulcha: Thicker, crisper Kulcha.
Punjabi Chole: Spicier, more flavorful Chole.
Vegetable Kulcha: Add grated vegetables (e.g., carrots, beets).

Nutritional Information (approximate):

Per serving (4-6 servings):
Calories: 400-500
Protein: 15-20g
Fat: 20-25g
Carbohydrates: 40-50g
Fiber: 5-7g

Health Benefits:
Rich in protein and fiber
Good source of vitamins and minerals
Can aid in digestion
Supports healthy blood sugar levels

Regional Variations:
North Indian Chole Kulcha: Spicier, more flavorful.
South Indian Chole Kulcha: Milder, with coconut.
East Indian Chole Kulcha: With mustard oil and spices.

Kulfi

Kulfi is a popular Indian ice cream made with milk, cream, sugar, and spices, frozen in a cylindrical shape.

Ingredients:
2 liters full fat milk
1 cup heavy cream
1 cup granulated sugar
1/4 teaspoon cardamom powder (elaichi)
1/4 teaspoon saffron threads (optional)
1/4 teaspoon pistachio or almond essence (optional)
Chopped nuts (e.g., pistachios, almonds) for garnish

Instructions:
1. Combine milk, cream, and sugar in a saucepan.
2. Heat until sugar dissolves.
3. Remove from heat, add cardamom powder and saffron threads (if using).
4. Let cool, then refrigerate.
5. Pour mixture into kulfi molds or a 9x13 inch baking dish.
6. Freeze for 6-8 hours or until set.
7. Unmold or scoop into cones or bowls.
8. Garnish with chopped nuts.

Tips:
Use full fat milk for a creamy texture.
Adjust sugar to desired sweetness.

Experiment with spices (e.g., cinnamon, nutmeg).
Add fruits (e.g., mango, strawberry) for unique flavors.

Variations:
Pistachio Kulfi: Add pistachio essence and chopped pistachios.
Saffron Kulfi: Increase saffron threads for vibrant color.
Mango Kulfi: Add pureed mango and cardamom powder.
Chocolate Kulfi: Add cocoa powder or melted chocolate.

Nutritional Information (approximate):

Per serving (4-6 servings):
Calories: 200-250
Protein: 5-7g
Fat: 10-12g
Carbohydrates: 25-30g
Fiber: 2-3g

Health Benefits:
Rich in calcium and protein
Good source of vitamins and minerals
Can aid in digestion
Supports healthy bone growth

Regional Variations:
North Indian Kulfi: Creamier and sweeter.
South Indian Kulfi: Coconutbased and lighter.
East Indian Kulfi: With jaggery and spices.

Kulfi Making Tips:
Use kulfi molds for traditional shapes.

Freeze mixture in a shallow metal pan for easier scooping.
Experiment with different spices and essences.
Add a pinch of salt to balance sweetness.
Serve immediately after unmolding.

Paya

Paya is a flavorful Indian stew made with goat trotters (or lamb/mutton legs), spices, and herbs.

Ingredients:
4-6 goat trotters (or lamb/mutton legs)
2 medium onions, chopped
2 medium tomatoes, chopped
2-3 cloves garlic, minced
1 teaspoon cumin seeds
1 teaspoon coriander powder
1 teaspoon garam masala
1 teaspoon turmeric
1 teaspoon red chili powder
Salt, to taste
2 tablespoons ghee or oil
2 tablespoons lemon juice
Chopped cilantro, for garnish

Instructions:
1. Clean and cut trotters into smaller pieces.
2. Heat ghee or oil, add cumin seeds, onions, and garlic.
3. Add chopped tomatoes, coriander powder, garam masala, turmeric, and red chili powder.
4. Add trotters, salt, and 2 cups of water.
5. Simmer for 1-2 hours or until the meat is tender.
6. Add lemon juice.

7. Garnish with chopped cilantro.

Tips:
Use tender goat trotters for best results.
Adjust spice level to desired heat.
Experiment with variations (e.g., adding potatoes, carrots).
Serve with naan or rice.

Variations:
Hyderabadi Paya: With coconut milk and spices.
Punjabi Paya: With ghee and garam masala.
South Indian Paya: With coconut and tamarind.
Vegetarian Paya: Replace trotters with mushrooms or vegetables.

Nutritional Information (approximate):

Per serving (4-6 servings):
Calories: 400-500
Protein: 30-40g
Fat: 20-25g
Carbohydrates: 20-25g
Fiber: 5-7g

Health Benefits:
Rich in protein and collagen
Good source of vitamins and minerals
Can aid in joint health
Supports healthy digestion

Regional Variations:
North Indian Paya: Spicier and more flavorful.

South Indian Paya: Coconut Based and lighter.
East Indian Paya: With mustard oil and spices.

Paya Serving Suggestions:
Serve with naan, rice, or roti.
Garnish with chopped cilantro and lemon wedges.
Pair with raita or salad.
Experiment with different spices and herbs.
Serve at special occasions or gatherings.

Ladoo

Ladoo is a popular Indian sweet made with gram flour, sugar, and ghee, often served during festivals and special occasions.

Ingredients:
2 cups gram flour (besan)
1 cup granulated sugar
1/2 cup ghee or unsalted butter
1/4 teaspoon cardamom powder (elaichi)
1/4 teaspoon saffron threads (optional)
Chopped nuts (e.g., almonds, pistachios) for garnish

Instructions:
1. Heat ghee or butter in a pan.
2. Add gram flour and roast until fragrant.
3. Add sugar, cardamom powder, and saffron threads (if using).
4. Mix well.
5. Add 1-2 tablespoons of water to form dough.
6. Shape into small balls (ladoos).
7. Garnish with chopped nuts.

Tips:
Use fine gram flour for a smooth texture.
Adjust sugar to desired sweetness.
Experiment with spices (e.g., cinnamon, nutmeg).
Store ladoos in an airtight container.

Variations:

Besan Ladoo: Classic gram flour ladoo.

Mothi Ladoo: With coconut and cardamom.

Boondi Ladoo: With fried gram flour droplets.

Rava Ladoo: With semolina and nuts.

Nutritional Information (approximate):

Per serving (4-6 servings):

Calories: 200-250

Protein: 5-7g

Fat: 10-12g

Carbohydrates: 25-30g

Fiber: 2-3g

Health Benefits:

Rich in protein and fiber

Good source of vitamins and minerals

Can aid in digestion

Supports healthy energy levels

Regional Variations:

North Indian Ladoo: More ghee and sugar.

South Indian Ladoo: Less ghee and more coconut.

East Indian Ladoo: With jaggery and spices.

Soan Papdi

Soan Papdi is a popular Indian dessert made with gram flour, sugar, and ghee, characterized by its flaky and crispy texture.

Ingredients:
1 cup gram flour (besan)
1/2 cup granulated sugar
1/4 cup ghee or unsalted butter
1/4 teaspoon cardamom powder (elaichi)
1/4 teaspoon saffron threads (optional)
Chopped nuts (e.g., almonds, pistachios) for garnish

Instructions:
1. Heat ghee or butter in a pan.
2. Add gram flour and roast until fragrant.
3. Add sugar, cardamom powder, and saffron threads (if using).
4. Mix well.
5. Add 1-2 tablespoons of water to form dough.
6. Knead dough.
7. Roll out dough into thin sheets.
8. Cut into diamond shapes.
9. Fry until golden brown.
10. Drain excess oil.
11. Garnish with chopped nuts.

Tips:
Use fine gram flour for a smooth texture.

Adjust sugar to desired sweetness.
Experiment with spices (e.g., cinnamon, nutmeg).
Store Soan Papdi in an airtight container.

Variations:

Besan Soan Papdi: Classic gram flour Soan Papdi.
Mysore Pak Soan Papdi: With coconut and cardamom.
Kesar Soan Papdi: With saffron and nuts.
Chocolate Soan Papdi: With cocoa powder and chocolate chips.

Nutritional Information (approximate):

Per serving (4-6 servings):
Calories: 250-300
Protein: 5-7g
Fat: 15-20g
Carbohydrates: 30-40g
Fiber: 2-3g

Health Benefits:
Rich in protein and fiber
Good source of vitamins and minerals
Can aid in digestion
Supports healthy energy levels

Regional Variations:
North Indian Soan Papdi: More ghee and sugar.
South Indian Soan Papdi: Less ghee and more coconut.
East Indian Soan Papdi: With jaggery and spices.

Jalebi

Jalebi is a popular Indian dessert made with fermented batter, deep fried and soaked in sugar syrup.

Ingredients:

For Batter:
1 cup all purpose flour
1/2 cup gram flour (besan)
1/4 teaspoon yeast
1/4 teaspoon salt
1/2 cup lukewarm water
1/4 cup ghee or oil
Cardamom powder (elaichi) for flavor

For Sugar Syrup:
1 cup granulated sugar
1 cup water
1/4 teaspoon cardamom powder (elaichi)
1/4 teaspoon saffron threads (optional)
Rose water or lemon juice for flavor

Instructions:

Batter Preparation:
1. Mix flour, gram flour, yeast, and salt.
2. Add lukewarm water and ghee or oil.

3. Knead smooth batter.
4. Ferment for 2-3 hours.

Frying Jalebi:
1. Heat oil in a deep frying pan.
2. Pour batter through a piping bag or a plastic bag with a hole.
3. Fry jalebi in spiral shapes until golden brown.
4. Drain excess oil.

Sugar Syrup Preparation:
1. Combine sugar, water, cardamom powder, and saffron threads (if using).
2. Heat until sugar dissolves.
3. Simmer until syrup thickens.

Assembly:
1. Soak fried jalebi in sugar syrup for 2-3 minutes.
2. Serve warm or chilled.

Tips:
Use fermented batter for crispy jalebi.
Adjust sugar syrup consistency.
Experiment with flavors (e.g., rose water, lemon juice).
Store jalebi in an airtight container.

Variations:
Crunchy Jalebi: With more gram flour.
Soft Jalebi: With more all purpose flour.
Fruit Jalebi: With fruit flavors (e.g., orange, strawberry).
Chocolate Jalebi: With cocoa powder and chocolate chips.

Nutritional Information (approximate):

Per serving (4-6 servings):
Calories: 250-300
Protein: 5-7g
Fat: 15-20g
Carbohydrates: 30-40g
Fiber: 2-3g

Health Benefits:
Rich in carbohydrates for energy
Good source of protein and fiber
Can aid in digestion
Supports healthy blood sugar levels

Paneer

Paneer is a popular Indian cheese made by curdling milk with lemon juice or vinegar.

Ingredients:
1 liter full-fat milk
1/2 cup lemon juice or vinegar
1/4 teaspoon salt
Cheesecloth or a clean cotton cloth

Instructions:
1. Boil milk in a large saucepan.
2. Reduce heat, add lemon juice or vinegar.
3. Stir gently until milk curdles.
4. Remove from heat, let it sit for 5-7 minutes.
5. Line a colander with cheesecloth or cloth.
6. Carefully pour curdled milk into cheesecloth.
7. Press excess liquid (whey) from the paneer.
8. Gather cloth edges, twist, and squeeze.
9. Flatten paneer underweight (e.g., plate).
10. Refrigerate for 2-3 hours.

Tips:
Use full-fat milk for creamy paneer.
Adjust lemon juice/vinegar for desired curdling.
Press the paneer gently to avoid breaking.
Store paneer in the refrigerator for up to 3 days.

Variations:
Malai Paneer: With cream and spices.
Smoked Paneer: With smoked flavor.
Herbed Paneer: With herbs (e.g., cilantro, parsley).
Spiced Paneer: With spices (e.g., cumin, coriander).

Nutritional Information (approximate):

Per serving (4-6 servings):
Calories: 200-250
Protein: 15-20g
Fat: 10-15g
Carbohydrates: 10-15g
Fiber: 0-1g

Health Benefits:
Rich in protein and calcium
Good source of vitamins and minerals
Supports healthy bone growth
Can aid in digestion

Regional Variations:
North Indian Paneer: Creamier and milder.
South Indian Paneer: Firmer and more crumbly.
East Indian Paneer: With jaggery and spices.

Using Paneer:
Palak Paneer: With spinach and spices.
Paneer Tikka Masala: With spices and tomato sauce.
Paneer Makhani: With butter and spices.

Paneer Biryani: With rice and spices.

Bai

Bai is a popular Mizo rice dish from Mizoram, India. It's a flavorful and aromatic preparation made with rice, meat or fish, and spices.

Ingredients:
2 cups rice
1 cup chicken or fish (boneless)
2 medium onions, chopped
2 medium tomatoes, chopped
2-3 cloves garlic, minced
1 tablespoon ginger paste
1 teaspoon Mizo chili powder (or substitute with cayenne pepper)
1 teaspoon coriander powder
1 teaspoon turmeric
Salt, to taste
2 tablespoons vegetable oil
2 cups water
Fresh cilantro, for garnish

Instructions:
1. Wash and soak rice for 30 minutes.
2. Drain rice, cook with 2 cups water until 70% done.
3. Heat oil, add onions, garlic, and ginger paste.
4. Add chicken or fish, cook until browned.
5. Add tomatoes, Mizo chili powder, coriander powder, turmeric, and salt.
6. Mix well, cook for 5 minutes.

7. Combine cooked rice with meat mixture.

8. Steam for 10-15 minutes or until rice is fully cooked.

9. Garnish with cilantro.

Tips:

Use short-grain rice for best results.

Adjust chili powder to desired heat.

Experiment with proteins (e.g., pork, beef).

Serve with Mizo chutney.

Variations:

Bai with Smoked Meat: Use smoked pork or chicken.

Bai with Fish: Use fish instead of chicken.

Vegetarian Bai: Replace meat with mushrooms or vegetables.

Nutritional Information (approximate):

Per serving (4-6 servings):

Calories: 400-500

Protein: 20-25g

Fat: 15-20g

Carbohydrates: 40-50g

Fiber: 2-3g

Health Benefits:

Rich in carbohydrates for energy

Good source of protein and fiber

Can aid in digestion

Supports healthy blood sugar levels

Regional Significance:

Bai is a staple dish in Mizoram, often served during special occasions and festivals.

Conclusion:

Mizoram Bai is a flavorful and aromatic rice dish that showcases the unique culinary traditions of Mizoram. With this simple recipe, you'll experience the authentic flavors of India's northeast.